IN VIA THE WAY

MW01247289

IN VIA THE WAY

Veejay Steele

Tampa, Florida

The content associated with this book is the sole work and responsibility of the author. Gatekeeper Press had no involvement in the generation of this content.

In Via The Way

Published by Gatekeeper Press
7853 Gunn Hwy., Suite 209
Tampa, FL 33626
www.GatekeeperPress.com

Copyright © 2023 by Veejay Steele
All rights reserved. Neither this book, nor any parts within it may be sold or reproduced in any form or by any electronic or mechanical means, including information storage and retrieval systems, without permission in writing from the author. The only exception is by a reviewer, who may quote short excerpts in a review.

Library of Congress Control Number: 2023945192

ISBN (paperback): 9781662941795
eISBN: 9781662941801

WARNING

PROPER USE OF 'THE WAY' WILL CAUSE ENERGY DRAIN!

★ YOU MAY BECOME VERY TIRED OR SLEEPY AFTER USING, THE WAY, FOR HOURS AT A TIME.

★ CREATING AND MAINTAINING A THOUGHT SO POWERFUL THAT THE UNIVERSE IS RESHAPED AROUND IT - REQUIRES WORK!

★ YOU AND THE DEVINE ENERGY ARE BOTH VERY HARD AT WORK.

THEREFORE, DRINK PLENTY OF WATER AND REST/RECHARGE WHEN YOU CAN.

IN VIA

(The Way)

Spiritual Praxis/Instruction Manual

[Introduction]

First, allow me to offer a little of myself and an opinion:

I am someone that doesn't put his complete trust or faith in any "system". What is a system? The American Heritage Dictionary defines a 'system' in several ways; here's a couple: (1) a group of interacting elements functioning as a complex whole. (2) a method; procedure.

In my opinion, no method or procedure is ever truly perfect. Furthermore, when you have a group of interacting elements functioning as a complex whole, that system can and most times will fail at some point, or at least to some degree. Concurrently, I only partially trust any system. Religion is typically such a system. Therefore, how can someone like me ever call himself religious? Well, like the word 'system,' religion is defined in more than one way. Again, from the American Heritage Dictionary, the term "religion" means: 1a) an organized system of beliefs and rituals centering on a supernatural being or beings, 1b) adherence to such a system, 2) a belief upheld or pursued with zeal and devotion.

According to those definitions, what I'm about to explain to you is something most people will quickly call religion or a system of faith, which is partially correct. However, though a method (a dogma – seemingly) will ultimately emerge from some of the instructions given; 'The Way' is still, in the end, just a cog; only one small part; another way of tapping into the universal power that connects all living things. - Being 'one small part' is the opposite of a system. How about religion? Once you become aware that 'The Way' works and delivers miracles to the 'truly connected', you will pursue 'The Way' with all the zeal and devotion of the most dedicated religious devotee. Still, 'The Way' is, at its core, merely instructions on _harnessing one's thoughts and focusing them with such precision, that the Universe itself, moves to align itself with those thoughts_. So, to eventually become a skilled practitioner, what will you need to do? Like a religion, will you need to believe? Have faith? Yes. At first. Eventually, you'll understand that 'The Way' is not a religion, is not a system, but only, **reality**. However, I'm getting ahead of myself. So, for right now, know this: Your pursuit of 'The Way,' like my own, will cause others to call it/see it as a religion. So for argument's sake, let's go ahead and call this a religion; and me a religious person. - I am Veejay Steele (Sylvester F. Steele, Jr. PKA Deca-Gon AKA -Gon), and this is, In Via, 'The Way.'

TABLE OF CONTENTS

Section I: PARTS

Upon inspection, you'll find three (marked A-C) major parts to In Via, also known as, The Way {this spiritual-praxis/religion/reality). The descriptions of all three parts (A, B, & C) are detailed below. - Please familiarize yourself with each one before proceeding.

(A) - God:

1. My father, Apostle/Bishop Sylvester F. Steele, Sr., used to say, "God is, thee spirit everywhere present". That is the correct short of it. However, I want you to picture the Yin-Yang symbol in your mind—dark and light swirled together. The Divine Energy that connects us, The Source we come from, what we're made up of, God, is both light and dark, both positive and negative, both creation and destruction, all at once.

2. What are good and evil then? Right and wrong? These are human concepts belonging to morality. Therefore, unlike light and dark, positive and negative, they don't follow a consistent pattern; they aren't constants.
For example, killing is considered bad/wrong. That's until it's done to eat, or in the name of justice, by officers, military, and the courts. Or it's God's WILL - to protect his/her people or punish the wicked. Killing is, in these instances, morally acceptable behavior. It can't be wrong whenever God does it. Pregnancy: this is a good thing, a rightful thing. If we're talking about giving birth and bringing new life into this world, then, of course, "morally speaking," most of us would say so. Does that remain true if a happily married woman conceived the child during an affair? Does it stay true if a happily married woman with a family {children with/by her husband) was raped? What if the expecting mother wasn't a woman at all but a ten-year-old girl? Morality is essential! It helps us to govern ourselves better. My point, however, is simply that the concepts of good and evil, right and wrong, are always in flux. We need to remember why that is - especially when discussing spirituality. Good and evil, right and wrong, have no place here.

3. The universal force, the source, the divine energy we are derived from, is both creation and destruction, both positive and negative, both light and dark. Therefore, the most skilled of our practitioners can move/flow between or touch both sides; while remembering to never be in the dark, the negative for too long, or else be consumed by it. Becoming someone we/society at large would consider evil {a horrible person). However, said practitioners can, when/if needed, if ever necessary, use/draw upon that energy to do whatever work needs to be done.
For instance, I'm from Pittsburgh, PA, where Castle Law allows me to use deadly force during an unlawful entry attempt; since 2011, it even includes the porch, deck, vehicles, and in some cases, places of employment. However, I'm currently living in California. Castle Law does exist here, just in a different manner. - I say all of that to say this:
I don't have a panic room in my house. Therefore, if someone were to break into my home and I killed them without hesitation, there's some chance that I'd be prosecuted. I could face murder charges; just for having the means and the will to do what's required to protect myself and my family. - With the sanctity of my home violated and no clue as to the real motivation or mindset of the perpetrators, I'd automatically call upon the full power of the destructive side of the force, of God, to assuredly do away with this potential threat to myself and my family. Touching the negative to bring about a more favorable situation for us.

Negative? To leave someone minus their life, to subtract it from them, is negative, even if it's God's will or done by God her/himself. But wrong? Or bad? Well, in the instance I've just described, that would be for a court to decide. Since it's an issue of morality - whatever we've (our society at large) chosen to believe is right or wrong, good or bad. God is neither. Still - ***AVOID THE NEGATIVE SIDE OF THE DIVINE ENERGY COMPLETELY THROUGHOUT YOUR LIFE, IF POSSIBLE***. *Since it is just that, NEGATIVE. The subtraction of things, of life. We all generally want positive things in our lives; pluses; increases; additions; in abundance. Touching the negative side, even for just a moment, WILL diminish you. If possible, always get what you need done, handled while staying positive.*

4. These human concepts: right/wrong, good/bad, are generally placed by most religions on God, personifying the Divine Energy; this typically is exacerbated further by the pronoun "He". However, God is NOT a person. God is neither good nor bad; neither male nor female. God IS the Divine Energy that connects all things. Energy is an infinite and eternal force. Nothing can

kill it, and it cannot die. All living things are bound to that force: this energy, Divine Energy, God. Flesh dies, but who you are can not. You/the energy derived (birthed, if you will) from the source is eternally connected to The Source. The eternal source is God. Now, although God is not a person, the part of the force most of us call upon for strength, aid, guidance, and wisdom is one of maternal essence. We generally expect that power to respond in a more nurturing sense. Thus, if you were going to personify God/The Source/The divine Energy, it would make more sense to use the pronoun "She" or the word "Mother." Though just like The Divine Energy is both positive and negative, it is also both Mother and Father in spirit/nature.

[The Divine Infinite Energy, The Source, that is both a positive and negative force, both creation and destruction, both Mother and Father, is - thee spirit everywhere present.]

(B) - You:

1. Who are you? I'm asking you, who are you? Go ahead and say your name. Say it aloud. Is that who you are? It's what *others* call you. It's one of the ways *they* know you. Right? Who would *they* say you are? Your race and gender are probably the first things out of *their* mouths when asked who YOU are. They could start with a physical description next: your height, approximate weight, and other physical attributes. Or, they could begin to describe your character: honest/dishonest, trustworthy/unreliable, truthful/a liar. Just about all of us possess an extensive range of emotions. However, someone who feels *they* know you may describe you expressing the emotional state *they* believe is typical for you: they are generally happy/sad, fun-loving/miserable. Or *they'd* speak first of your mannerism: they are usually very silly/serious. In whatever way *others* see you, maybe that's who you are. - - - It isn't.

2. Your name, any of the proper descriptions of you, whether physical, mental or emotional, not even your physical body, is who you are. Who you are, is the energy that dwells within you. You are the divine energy that operates the body which houses it. Who you are is immortal. Immortal Divine Energy is generally considered the very makeup of God/Thee Creator. You then are God.

3. You ARE derived from and are a unique part of the Immortal Divine Infinite Energy, The Source, God. You, like your fingerprints, carry a unique signature. Though having a unique energy signature, you ARE joined/one with the Divine Energy which expands throughout a universe of incalculable size and connects everything. You ARE NOT simply flesh, blood, and bone. You ARE a constant force, part of an energy that cannot die, cannot perish and will exist forever. - Let it be understood by you that: derived from, yet connected to/joined with, makes you the same. You are GOD. God is YOU.

(C) - Connection:

1. Where is God? On high - atop a mountain? Beyond the sky? Beyond the stars? In the heavens? Please allow me to reiterate: The Divine Energy is PRESENT EVERYWHERE. Here's another old saying/teaching from my father, "Where you are, God is... where God is, you are". Can you imagine that? Being EVERYWHERE that's ANYWHERE, all at the same time? You are here, yet, you are also there. Thereon inhabited planets that the beings of the earth have yet to find. Here with me as I type these words, just as I am there with you as you read them now - because we are all part of the Divine Energy/God. Which, again, is present everywhere. Being part of The Source, this is the connection we share.

2. Remember that we are talking about and dealing with energy. An energy that is present everywhere; one that we're born from, and therefore, part of; the power you exist as beyond your physical make-up. Now, if you are part of an energy present everywhere, you are connected to everything and everyone, everywhere. Again, it's because you are God, and God is You. God is the Divine Energy you are derived from/part of, making you the same.
Is there any kind/sort of uniqueness beyond your physical body? Yes. You have a unique energy signature. Though you are part of the source, you are still one of a kind.
- Look right now at the palm of your hand. For this example, your palm will be The Source/God/The Divine Energy/that from which you have been derived. With your unique energy signature, you will be your index/first digit (if not counting the thumb as a finger). You are part of The Source, yet very unique, especially when compared to your pinky/little/the last digit, also 'connected' to The Source, and just as unique. They can move independently of one another. They are different in physical shape and size, both in length and width. Their interphalangeal creases (the lines running across the finger where the bones connect/where it bends) are different. They have entirely different grip strengths. - Every finger, all of us, unique, yet still attached to the source.

3. It may be an oxymoron; however, your unique energy signature makes us indivisible.
- Allow me to use an analogy that may help to clarify my point:
We all have a unique energy signature or frequency, which is a way to tune into our particular channel—likened to that of FM or AM *radio stations with* separate tuning frequencies or channels. They are all part of *radio wave*s {a type of electromagnetic radiation).
Your energy signature is unique; you are an individual radio station. However, whether AM or FM, positive or negative, we are all carried on/derived from electromagnetic radiation/radio waves/The Source/The Divine Energy/God. We are unique stations/channels—from/connected to/part of the same source.

Section II: ASSEMBLY

Before beginning the first step, you must understand three things:
- ➤ *1st. The steps mentioned/described below are all that are necessary for assembly.*
- ➤ *2nd. This assembly can be done anywhere and at any time.*
- ➤ *3rd. A congregation and a designated place to worship are NOT required.*

Step 1 -
So, only after reading this manual in its entirety: sit back; stand still or lay still; close your eyes - if you can; leave them open - if you must; take a few deep breaths; then callout (aloud using your voice, or in silence using only thought) to The Divine Energy; to The Universe; to The Source; to The Creator; to God; to Her. * Here now are the words I speak (slowly and methodically) to establish my connection, "Almighty Mother... Mother of all creation, please hear me now, Mother, please hear me now...".

Step 2 -
Once a connection has been established, a link strengthened by emotion—more on that later, commune with Her without fear. - You should know that nothing you can say is "wrong." Therefore, allow ONLY THE TRUTH to leave your lips as words or your mind as a thought. - Try to choose your words as wisely as possible; know their meaning before speaking them/thinking them. Let every word you say or think come from your heart. In other words, be confident every

 statement made and anything and everything asked for is in complete and absolute sincerity. - If what was said is *true*, it remains so during the second assembly, the third, fourth, and so on. - Focus. - Picture the words you're speaking or thinking - in action. Picture the movement of, The Universe, of The Divine Energy, of The Force, of God as She goes to work for you. Picture Her every action as you speak/think/call The Divine Energy into action.

Step 3 -
When bringing the assembly to a close, it is customary for most Americans (being that we are *mostly* Christian) to say, "Amen." However, I close by thanking Her (Giving Thanks); and follow that with, "I love you" (Taking Leave).

Giving Thanks:

Besides thanking Her for my life, health, and strength - I am as specific as possible when giving thanks.

I thank Her (The Creator/The Universe/The Divine Energy/The Force/The Collective/The Source) for the individual victories she's awarded me—successes due to and made possible by wholly harnessed, concentrated, specific thought - from me - shared by Her - amplified then, immeasurably.

*Shared thought. *Shared performance of the task.

I thank Her for the miracles performed.

My definition of a miracle is this: whenever I've come against situations that I believe, in my best estimation, are impossible to change, circumstances that would take a miracle to render results as I desire them. Yet, results are provided, in time, precisely as I've prayed/decreed them be. → That is the witnessing of a miracle to me.

I thank her for having always been and forever being with me.

I thank her for loving me.

Taking Leave:

"Amen" is an interjection that means: "So be it." That makes it the proper choice for closing *prayer*. Prayer means that you have expressed your thoughts to The Universe, The Creator, The Divine Energy, to God, and told Her what you need, want, desire, or hope for, then ended that prayer with "So be it" — better known as "Amen." However, when using The Way, the assembly is more like a personal conversation. A conversation between you and The Divine Energy/The Mother/God. One where YOU speak, SHE listens, and thoughts/things revealed to your mind (**the revelation[s]**) … are Her speaking back to you.

When ending a conversation with Divine Energy, considerably more important than a parent, a spouse, a child, or any loved one - you should feel compelled to make known your most authentic feelings (your LOVE) for Her. Therefore, I believe the phrase "I love you" is the ONLY way to close/temporarily end the conversation.

Section III: OPERATION

➔ *Now that you're familiar with and understand the PARTS...*
➔ *Now that you know how to start and finish the ASSEMBLY...*
➔ *It's time to fully understand how this works, how to use and operate, The Way.*

First comes the hard part.

--- Remove ALL DOUBT from your mind. ---

To do so, understand as clearly as possible that all you've read thus far is Universal Reality. - 'The Way' works because... well... honestly... it's just the way it is. - It's the way things are. - It's the way things operate. - Know that. - Accepting this reality will allow you to become a powerful practitioner immediately.

If you're a woman, you do indeed have a slight advantage. Your connection to God is stronger than that of a man. The reason is that the link itself is strengthened by emotion. Ever notice that in times of mental anguish, your prayers/your decrees become more powerful? That they seem to be received by the Divine Energy, forthwith? That the responses/answers to your prayers happen more rapidly? Emotion strengthens the connection — the more potent the feeling, the stronger the bond.

Human males and females are equally emotional beings at birth. However, not long after, boys are taught to lessen their emotions and become more cerebral - moving through life using only their intelligence. Nowadays, these same parents give similar instructions to females, except they are permitted, expected, and encouraged to be emotional. Again, emotion strengthens the connection.

> *[Allow me to explain this in a slightly different manner. So, say your 'connection' is like being on the phone; YOU on one end, and GOD on the other. You're conversing, not about anything in particular, just chatting. Your discussion is ongoing, but both parties have difficulty hearing one another. The connection seems weak and even delayed. Well, contrarily, that connection is ten times stronger when you're in ANY emotional state. The conversation is crystal clear, with no problems being heard by either party.]*

Therefore, allow yourself to feel. Don't be afraid to be overcome with emotion. It doesn't matter whether or not the connection's made for casual conversation or if it was created to place a 911 call. Either way, you want the link as strong as possible. So get in touch - first - with your emotions.

It's all about becoming "truly connected". The more closely connected you are to the source, the easier it'll be to shape the universe as you desire, as only God can. Removing all doubt and allowing yourself to be emotional brings you closer to becoming "truly connected".

Remember all that you've learned thus far.

You are NOT to be subservient in any; way, shape, or form. Be at ease with your ability (by way of The Creator) to shape the universe as you see fit. Even if you've just placed a 911 call from an emotional state of pure distress, EXPECT the response to that call to deliver the victory you seek.

You are God, and God is You.
Understand the symbiosis. Allow it to become ONENESS.
Then you are TRULY CONNECTED.

The Assembly: other than when it's just a conversation for conversation's sake - it first tells the story; details the situation to make it clear to you and the Divine Energy what the issue is. That conversation lasts only as long as needed to make that clear. You should have that conversation at least a couple of times daily. Everything else you do in the meantime is detailed here:

- To use The Way, you must do all these things. But, what I instruct you to do next is something you must do as often as possible. All day, every day, if it were possible. Until the victory you seek - is yours, the miracle you want to be performed – is done.
- The Assembly: It was likely a very lengthy conversation. Whatever it may have been about, break it down now. Sum up that conversation into as few words as possible. Can you get it down to eight words? Five? Four? Or even just two? Try VERY hard to do so. Two words now that, if enacted, would deliver for you the victory you seek, the miracle you want fulfilled. What I just described is - harnessing your thoughts.
  - Let's say you got it down to ten words in two sentences. Then, I want you to think about or repeat those two sentences again and again. Doing so is how you focus your thoughts.
  - You were very careful in choosing each word in those sentences. So already, those two short sentences have power. They sum up your whole conversation (The Assembly) with The Almighty. - Feelings & thoughts, harnessed.
  - You're repeating them {the two sentences) while envisioning The Divine Energy doing the work to make it happen. You don't even know how long you've been repeating them and seeing it all come to fruition in your mind. Has it been minutes or hours? Your thoughts are focused with precision. As a result, those two sentences/your ideas are called into being; they are used to shape a new reality created by The Almighty & you.

KNOW THAT:

- Due to the **complete mental focus** on that <u>thought</u>, on those few words, from a **doubtless mind** -

- On account of the **meticulous selection of the words** used and the **cutting down of those words** to just a few - giving <u>the thought pinpoint precision</u> -

- For **speaking those words** to the Universe (while envisioning The Divine Energy moving/working to make it happen) in an almost **endless repetition** -

  - the universe itself is NOW moving to align with that thought.

This isn't fantasy.
This is the universal truth. This is simply *reality*.
THIS IS **THE WAY**

Section IV: TROUBLESHOOTING

[part 1]*****A QUESTION (Q) and ANSWERS (A)*****

Q: I've followed all the instructions to the letter, but it seems it isn't working — what am I doing wrong?

There may be a few reasons for this. The answers below may help.

A: Do your BEST to listen & follow her instructions.
Remember, the thoughts revealed to your mind (***the revelation[s]***) during and after you've conversed with The Mother is Her way of communicating with you. Follow Her instructions to the letter. *Typically, if your *precision, focused thought* isn't positive enough, She will give you another set of words or sentences to use. Positive forces are the strongest of Her forces, yielding lasting, permanent results. STAY POSITIVE.

A: Know the difference between CHANGE and MODIFY.
When using The Way, it's best to understand that most things CAN NOT be "changed". Usually, once something/anything is created, it is what it is. However, though the degrees of which will vary, "modification" is always possible. For instance, the metaphorical speakers accompanying this "audio system" should not be changed into anything else. They were created as 'speakers'. However, the sound/the music they produce… well, what if you *amplified* the bass? What if you left every sound coming through the speakers the same, except you *increased* the treble? The sound that the speakers produce, the music being heard by them would be different. Making this slight modification will have effectively 'changed' things.
     Always consider the difference between 'change' and 'modify' before using The Way.
- NOTE: There is usually more than one definition per word. The synonyms *'change'* and *'modify'* share one: *to alter*. Here's where their meanings differ:

Change: to exchange for or replace by another
Modify: to make or become less extreme, severe, or strong

A: Be patient.
You've understood the parts thoroughly; your assembly(s) couldn't have gone any better; you're operating The Way like a seasoned practitioner. Yet, you're not hearing the sweet music of victory you've been expecting to hear. Well, the task is monumental. The universe itself is being moved to align with your thoughts - through the power of the Divine Energy - this takes time. However, if you're at the point of repeating the few words/sentences that sum up your conversations (assembly) with The Almighty, the process is MOST CERTAINLY underway. Stay with it. Don't stop. The miracle you want/need performed will be. The victory you seek will be yours. Don't doubt. Know this: it IS at hand.

SPECIAL NOTE
DO NOT STOP USING THE WAY, EVEN WHEN THE MIRACLE YOU WANT AND THE VICTORY
YOU SEEK ARE COMING TO FRUITION.
- IT'S NOT OVER UNTIL IT'S OVER! -

A: <u>Beware of opposing forces.</u>
We live in a world that has become more virtually social than at any other time in human history. A world where "virtually" people share just about all of their business {opinions, affairs, matters, things, cases, circumstances, situations, events, incidents, happenings, occurrences, episodes, developments, news) with "friends," friends of friends, associates, colleagues, acquaintances, and the like. There isn't even much discretion used nowadays. Example: "Here at work, and just took an extra-long potty break…". Most people are open to sharing their most intimate ongoings and secrets online. Especially if they believe the others they share them with will aid them in their cause. We want to think that "friends" and maybe even friends of friends will have our back. Perhaps this makes me a cynic, though I believe it is an unpleasant truth; most people, even some of those closest to you, secretly don't want you to succeed. Their negative thoughts will interfere with the victory you seek, the miracle you require. Therefore, if possible, keep the details about your use of The Way to yourself. *"Play it close to the chest"* {a correct and helpful idiom in this circumstance).

- Negative thoughts are the only form in which an *enemy* exists; outside yourself.

Speaking of interference -

[part 2]*****INTERFERENCE (outside and inside)*****

Somewhat detrimental to the victory you seek, the miracle you want to be performed, your use of The Way, is outside and inside interference. Let's examine both of these.

<u>Outside Interference</u> - this could be when you're attempting to connect with The Almighty for assembly amidst the common everyday noises or ongoings of your family/household. If you're a parent: bedtime may very well be the only break you get when it comes to your job as a mother/father. Or, you're driving in moderate to heavy traffic while attempting the assembly. Alone time may strictly consist of your solo commute to and from work.
- Encountering these and other conditions, activities, noises, and disruptions not of your own making are considered outside interference.

<u>Inside Interference</u> - could be classified as when, during your assembly, you begin to think or daydream of something other than what you're discussing. When, in other words, you can't seem to stop the most random thoughts from propagating in your consciousness.
- These occurrences or anything similar to these; disruptions of your own making are considered inside interference.

So what should you do about interference? Consider the course of action described below.

PRACTICALLY
BEING WELL RESTED… ALONE…
SOMEWHERE WITH VERY LITTLE TO NO BACKGROUND NOISE…
SOMEWHERE THERE'S LITTLE TO ZERO CHANCE OF YOU BEING INTERRUPTED…
THIS WOULD BE THE IDEAL TIME AND PLACE FOR AN ASSEMBLY
[Specifically, an ideal time & place would be directly after showering/bathing, before doing anything else.]

Furthermore, being well-rested and having a strong desire for the occurrence of the miracle you want, the victory you seek, will help you keep your focus.

The stronger your desire, the more powerful your conviction, and the higher your emotion - the better your connection. Better is your conversation. It's less likely that any kind/type of interference could be significant enough to disrupt your assembly.

Whatever you're using The Way for, if you want it badly enough - INTERFERENCE - of ANY KIND could hardly ever be an issue.
- You'll drive to work in traffic, but since you're alone and want the victory you seek, the miracle you need, you'll speak aloud to The Mother while still focusing on the road.
- If you want your victory badly enough, you will find the time and a place in your home to be alone and speak aloud to The Divine Energy, to The Mother.

Speaking aloud - helps keep your mind on the words you are using, the message you must deliver, and the point you're trying to convey. **Don't be afraid to speak aloud**. It helps block both outside and inside interference.

Again, how badly/how much do you want your miracle, your victory awarded to you? Wanting it badly enough will cause you to: find time alone; speak aloud during assembly; keep your train of thought; wait and remember to converse after you're well-rested; never try talking, knowing you're sleepy, tired, or exhausted.

Wanting it badly enough, having no desire stronger than the one for the miracle you seek, the victory you need - will help you overcome some actual and all potential interference.

— About exhaustion —

[part 3]*****DRAIN (physical, mental & emotional)*****

A warning came with this manual. It read:
*Proper use of The Way will cause energy drain! You may become very tired or sleepy after using The Way for hours at a time. Creating and maintaining a thought so powerful that the universe is reshaped around it - requires work! You and The Divine Energy are both **very hard at work**. - Therefore, drink plenty of water and rest/recharge when you can.*
- Heed the WARNING! - It will help you with most of the physical drain that occurs. However, properly using The Way isn't the only cause of depletion. There may be more ominous reasons. Let's examine these and rectify them if they exist.

Since physical drain will hinder your use of The Way, it is detrimental to the victory you seek and the miracle you want; therefore, you must stop it. However, you've heeded the warning that came with this manual. Thus, you know that properly using The Way isn't the cause of your physical drain. So what is it?
You've been using The Way, day in and day out, for weeks. The victory you seek, the miracle you want, has yet to be fully realized. - So you've grown weary. - The physical drain you're experiencing results from an occurring mental or emotional one.

<u>Mental Drain</u> - is a common side effect of prolonged use of, In Via. However, a more inauspicious reason for the occurrence of this side effect may also begin to present itself. First, let's discuss 'mental drain' as it results from proper, prolonged use of In Via; and, as it must be, how it's remedied.

A constant positive focus on the victory you seek/the miracle you need while chanting, quietly or aloud, the few words/sentences that sum up your assembly with The Divine Energy means — on top of all the work by your mind to produce every correct response and every thought needed to get you through your day - there's now much more work - an even greater demand of the mind required. *You've given the order for your mind to <u>dwell relentlessly</u> upon the few words or sentences that have become *the super-concentrated thought* that will alter your current reality.*

- [The Remedy] Treatment of the side effect (mental drain) in this case is a simple two-step (a/b) process: Expectation & Habituation.
(a) **expectation**: almost anything and everything is better handled by you if you expect it/see it coming.
(b) **habituation**: simply get used to it. Get used to the extra work. - Like lifting weights; as muscles grow and strength increases, what seemed heavy before is no longer so.

Here is the full disclosure of the more sinister cause/reason for the mental drain. - Simply put, it is the result of the war raging inside your mind—the war of Intelligence versus Faith.

*Discussed below in TROUBLESHOOTING [part 4].

<u>Emotional Drain</u> - can occur due to prolonged use of, In Via. Therefore, it too may be considered a side effect; just like a mental drain, you must remedy it. Also, like a mental drain, there may be another reason for its occurrence. One more difficult to cure. So first, let's discuss emotional drain as it results from prolonged use of, In Via (The Way).

The use of In Via (The Way) is about delivering for you the victory you seek, the miracle you want/need to be implemented, and a personally positive result. However, it typically means that you also have to dwell upon what has caused you to use it in the first place. That's usually something negative. Something upsetting to you. Asking for victory over it means you have to think of *it* or on *it*. Dwelling upon sad, bad, negative things is emotionally draining. As previously stated, touching the negative, even for just a moment, will diminish you. In this case, because doing so is a must, this is how we fight back and successfully combat it.

- [The Remedy] Treatment of the side effect (emotional drain) in this case is as follows: **USE AS DIRECTED**. Yes, it's that simple. Though you must think for a moment about what you're using The Way for - dwelling upon the negative situation you're seeking victory over - it is only for that moment. The rest of the time, you are either in an assembly with The Almighty, where you speak to Her about all the positive movements you'd like Her to make on your behalf. Or you are chanting/repeating your super concentrated, wholly positive thought that is reshaping the universe. The point is, EVERYTHING you do after the initial review of why you're doing it … is FULLY POSITIVE.
- - In the words of the late Father Divine (Reverend Major Jealous Divine), "*You got to accentuate the positive and eliminate the negative*". - Accentuating the positive will indeed stifle the negative. So, USE AS DIRECTED.

However, the mental and emotional drain may also be agents of a much more significant problem. Let's discuss it.

Here is the greatest threat to the successful use of The Way —

[part 4]*****INTELLIGENCE versus FAITH*****

If you're reading this, you're literate; if you can comprehend it…
Ask yourself, just getting through all the rigmarole of everyday life, is there anything of greater use to you than your intelligence?
- *Adaptation is currently and typically the marker used to gauge intelligence. It's all about the adjustments you make to deal with your environment or the adjustments you make to your domain to contend.*
However, we aren't always so adaptable. Ironically, our intelligence doesn't always allow us to be.

> **Now, we could spend hours here discussing the numerous theories composed by respected experts, throughout history, on the subject of intelligence — on or about what exactly it is. There would be pages upon pages to read right now if we discussed, even briefly, just a few of those respected opinions on the subject.**

Doing some individual research on the subject of intelligence may be beneficial. We will discuss it as if you have some knowledge of the matter, which most of us probably have. So, with that said, let's get right to it.

When examining it from an intellectual standpoint, this manual was written to help you do something *impossible*. Now, deeming anything *impossible* is (usually) a direct result of using intelligence, specifically, deduction {⅓ of the main components of logical thinking). It takes *intelligence* to deduce a situation correctly. - If something has been deemed *impossible*, it has been done, most likely by finding data to support that conclusion—-through deduction. Furthermore, most intelligent people do believe that some things are simply *impossible*. A conclusion, once reached, halts adaptation.
- Here is the American Heritage Dictionary definition of impossible.
Impossible: *1. Not capable of existing or happening. 2. Having little likelihood of happening or being accomplished. 3. Unacceptable 4. Not capable of being dealt with or tolerated; objectionable.*
Therefore, if you believe what you've read is *impossible* - your intelligence keeps you from using this innate ability, accepting a universal truth, and recognizing the reality of The Way things are. I say to you — if your intelligence is hindering you from processing all of this as *truth* and is instead leaving you to believe it all to be *impossible,* then at this moment, you need to turn away from your *intelligence* and embrace your *faith*. Right now, have *faith* that what you've read is real, is true. Have *faith* that it will work if you only follow the instructions.
Use The Way strictly through *faith*. Then, after you've received the victory you seek, and after the miracle you want to be performed has been, remember then - all of the details that lead up to it happening. Use, at that time, your *intelligence* to truthfully write a report—write a detailed account of the miracle as it happened. Write it down and read it again and again. Then, ask yourself, how — how is this possible? No longer will you believe The Way to be instructions on doing the impossible. You'll know it's simply The Way things are; it's a universal truth; it's a reality.

I mentioned earlier a more sinister reason for the mental drain. Well, it's not that *intelligence* is evil or something sinister. However, the **war** raging in your mind between your intellect and *faith*, like any war, is harmful. War, even with justifiable reasons, will lead to significant harm in some way; therefore, it can be considered sinister.

-   If your *intelligence* is causing you to conclude that this manual is filled with instructions on doing the *impossible*, thus you can't accept it.
-   However, you desperately need a miracle performed and a victory you *believe* could be awarded through the use of The Way.
-   Then, in your mind, is the beginning/the makings of a **war** that will rage between your *intelligence* and your *faith*.

The outcome/the victory you're seeking that led to your use of The Way in the first place, it/that will be the true casualty of this war. Along with the feeling, you could also be one due to mental, emotional, and physical drains.

A war sustained for a significant time comes at a high cost. In this case, the charge is - your energy. It's what's fueling this war. Precisely, all the mental energy needed for comprehension of this manual to support your faith; is in direct opposition with the mental energy required to develop reasons, to generate the ideas, reasons & ideas that will lend credence to the intelligence used to label The Way *impossible*. With so much mental energy being used to support both sides of this war - your overall energy - your lifeforce itself, is in danger of draining.

Let us remember that who you are, is energy. Since energy cannot die, you, the actual/true you, never will; contrarily, your flesh can.

A certain amount of energy is used to maintain the body/to stimulate all of its functions; that power is directly responsible for assisting the body in preserving life. Thus, we can only afford so much drain of that energy.
-Mental drain, resulting from mental conflict - is causing a severe physical drain.-

The war between your intelligence and your faith isn't just responsible for the mental drain you're experiencing; it's also the catalyst for the emotional drain that may be occurring. - Believe me, your weariness has everything to do with your intelligence.
Yes, it's been a tough road, long and hard. The more time passes, the more difficult it becomes to stay positive, to believe that The Way is working. That's because, during that time, you have been thinking about the particular reasons it shouldn't be working - and why this specific victory is *impossible* to achieve. Of course, if you think about it hard enough, you may come up with many reasons why The Way, in your particular instance, shouldn't work. These thoughts on/about how and why you can not win your victory are depressing. They leave you weary and with a sense of dread, which directly contrasts with the conclusion of your use of The Way. You are suffering from an emotional drain, and your intelligence is directly responsible. You are choosing to think about the tangible things you are up against and conclude that they can keep you from the victory you seek. If turning away from your intelligence and embracing your faith isn't enough—if it has proven too difficult for you to do, then instead, do this:

USE YOUR INTELLIGENCE TO LEND SUPPORT TO YOUR FAITH.

Here's how —

By now, enough has happened that you can pick out some of the positive things that have occurred during your use of The Way. No matter how small or seemingly insignificant, FOCUS NOW ON THEM. Even if they could be explained away, they still HAPPENED. Think hard about them now; they support your faith. Yet, they require your intelligence to think on them; to admit and recognize that they happened. - They are things that occurred that are positive during your time of struggle and use of The Way; they then lend full support to your faith; evidence that The Way is working.

- Now, you've just collected data to support the argument, also known as a deduction, effectively using your intelligence to defend your faith.

The war must end, and your faith must be the victor.
Having your intelligence go from an adversarial role to a supportive one guarantees this.

[part 5]*****TEST (trials & tribulations)*****

Through God, faith, and The Way, victory is assured/guaranteed. However, just as sure are the tests {trials and tribulations) you will face/go through as you make your way on the path.

➔ *In Via is, in part: about using the limitless power and capabilities each of us is naturally endowed with (and connected to even before our physical existence) to perform great works.*
➔ *And though tapping into and using this power (becoming ONE with The Almighty) will become easier over time… reshaping the universe itself (the process of creation) is NEVER a simple task.*

USUALLY insisted upon by The Divine Energy, by God, by The Mother, by The Universe, is a gestation period right after the initial conception, typically followed by a long, very strenuous labor.

Understand: if you want the victory you seek badly enough, not only should you be willing to go through this but be you, man or woman, you WILL - go through this. Your desire for and commitment to what you claim to want and need WILL be tested during this period. It will sometimes be like seeing sharp curves in the road ahead; thus, you can adjust as you approach them. Seeing it means you'll be able to, or have time to, prepare for the *test* yet to come. However, there are other times that you can't and won't see them coming, times that they will arrive/occur without warning, like a pop quiz. In either of these cases, there exists only ONE correct answer, only ONE solution, and only ONE way to solve every problem to pass these *tests* correctly. Yet applying the answer could be as difficult as taking/enduring the *test*. That's because the only thing you can do, the only solution to passing every *test* as they come, is to - GO HARDER!

- *DEFINITION -*
  - *__GO HARDER:__ 1) increase all efforts, 2) give a situation more time, attention, and focus than what you gave previously, 3) push past/through the pain {consciously endure all suffering from an increased will to win while going forward), 4) ultimately chose to believe that there's no way for you to slow or stop in your pursuit of victory. 5) STOP and DO NOTHING.*

a) When all seems lost —
b) When the desire to work for the victory you've been seeking is gone —
c) When the hurt and pain of seeing it all (seemingly) fall apart, have you doubting your faith; have you ready to abandon The Way and turn away from God —

GO HARDER!

You are being *tested* — a, b, and c above are just some of the things you can and should expect to occur and endure during this *trial* period. So **DON'T FAIL**.
NEVER throw in the proverbial towel. Instead -
GO HARDER:

- Make a conscious effort to stick to it, to see it/this through.
- Don't let or allow opposing forces to win against you.
- Even if YOU can't see any room, any way to still achieve victory… WORK! - Work that much harder to make it happen.

  (increase the __intensity__ of your assemblies; chant/speak your PFP {precision focused words/phrase] even more often)

While you labor and deal with the *tribulations* of being a dedicated, In Via practitioner, understand: pain happens; pain comes; pain and suffering occur, but you can, will, and must endure. - It is all simply part of the process. - Creation is not typically without labor; labor is rarely without pain.

Now if and when you must <u>GO EVEN HARDER STILL</u> … *know* this, and then *do* this:

First… *know* this…

Hurt, pain, and suffering are real and mighty things. Sometimes, the hurt causes pain that can/will seem to be genuinely insufferable. It can cause you to look for anyway and be willing to do anything to stop it. At that moment, know that you should take a second and breathe while remembering that you are part of a more significant, all-powerful/almighty force.

Now… *do* this…

Since you've reached the point where you've needed to take a moment, you must, right now, GO EVEN HARDER STILL; do the most powerful thing you can do. Right now, STOP… and DO ABSOLUTELY NOTHING. Right now, be still. "Let go and let God". Know that you must and will be here to see this through—no more dwelling on the negative. You'll recognize the end when it arrives; since unmistakable/unequivocal, and definite is your victory. Until then, while being still mentally & spiritually - relax. Smile now, with complete confidence that you've done ALL that you could, and now [since allowing The Mother to take over for you - fully], your victory is won. — THE OMNIPOTENT is *moving* in HER FULL MAGNIFICENCE and will TRIUMPH for YOU.

[part 6]*****BUYERS REMORSE (careful what you wish for)*****

"And pray what would satisfy you?" asked the stranger. "Merely for the curiosity of the thing, I should be glad to know."

Midas paused and meditated. He felt a presentiment that this stranger, with such a golden lustre in his good-humored smile, had come hither with both the power and the purpose of gratifying his utmost wishes. Now, therefore, was the fortunate moment, when he had but to speak, and obtain whatever possible, or seemingly impossible thing, it might come into his head to ask. So he thought, and thought, and thought, and heaped up one golden mountain upon another, in his imagination, without being able to imagine them big enough. At last, a bright idea occurred to King Midas. It seemed really as bright as the glistening metal which he loved so much.

Raising his head, he looked the lustrous stranger in the face.

"Well, Midas," observed his visitor, "I see that you have at length hit upon something that will satisfy you. Tell me your wish."

"It is only this," replied Midas. "I am weary of collecting my treasures with so much trouble, and beholding the heap so diminutive, after I have done my best. I wish everything that I touch to be changed to gold!"

The stranger's smile grew so very broad, that it seemed to fill the room like an outburst of the sun, gleaming into a shadowy dell, where the yellow autumnal leaves--for so looked the lumps and particles of gold--lie strewn in the glow of light.

"The Golden Touch!" exclaimed he. "You certainly deserve credit, friend Midas, for striking out so brilliant a conception. But are you quite sure that this will satisfy you?"

"How could it fail?" said Midas.

"And will you never regret the possession of it?"

"What could induce me?" asked Midas. "I ask nothing else, to render me perfectly happy."

"Be it as you wish, then," replied the stranger...

←above (written under 'part 6, BUYERS REMORSE…') is an excerpt from "'The Golden Touch' - A Wonder-Book for Girls and Boys (1851)" by American author Nathaniel Hawthorne

Just as the Greek God Dionysus (the Roman God Bacchus) bestowed the 'golden touch' upon King Midas, turning his desire into reality, so will The Mother grant you your highest thoughts and desires. Through, In Via/The Way, She will make actual that which you have labored so long to bring into existence. However, unlike in the story of King Midas, a bath in the river Pactolus will not undo Her blessing. There will be NO undoing the miracle She has performed for you, the victory She has won for you. Through, In Via/The Way, once She has created something, once She has made it so, you can not make it otherwise.

Most things, no matter how strongly you desire them, are not and will not be worth using In Via. Likewise, you shouldn't use In Via to alter most occurrences, situations, or troubles you may face.

➔ You believe whatever you've decided to use In Via for is worth all the time, energy, focus, thought, pain, and suffering you will spend and endure. You genuinely feel that it is. You think it, feel it, more potent than anything else you've ever felt. You're so confident that it's worth using In Via that you'd sacrifice all you are and all you hold dear for the fruition of the miracle you seek - the victory you seek.

Yet, in most cases, you'd be utterly mistaken.

The use of In Via should be an absolute last resort. You should explore, in earnest, all other options; then, to the best of your abilities, perform the very deepest of thought about your future. See as clearly as you can what your life will be like if you simply accept things as they are. Choose *now* to see the bigger picture, and if you're honest with yourself, you may realize you'd be better off reaching the destination God has set for you.

The Mother behind the wheel, as She has always been, will not steer you wrong and has a predetermined destination for you both. You are, however, allowed to grab the wheel and share the responsibility of the drive; even altering the course and the destination She previously set. This is your right. However, as I just said, The Mother had predetermined your heading and would always steer you right. Thus, it is usually best to simply trust in the Lord; trust the course She has set; trust in your ability to endure the journey; trust the road leading to your destination, no matter how bumpy, no matter how rough it may *seem*.

Remember, most things can only be *modified,* not changed. Therefore, ask for the strength to accept that which you CAN NOT *change.*

>*Keep in mind —
>In Via is a labor-intensive practice, especially initially. One that works yet requires much of your time, effort, energy, and some stress, strain, pain, and suffering with and during its use. **It is *not* prayer**. God answers prayers simply for the asking. In Via, it isn't "Ask, and you shall receive". In Via is the creation process—creating a new reality as YOU desire. It is the practice of harnessing your thoughts; focusing them; having them be shared with/by The Divine Energy of All Creation; thus, having The Universe move to align itself with those thoughts - creating a *new* reality. Therefore, its use should be even more painstakingly and heavily considered than the most responsible parents' decision to bring new life into this world - as the result of doing so is just as permanent.

Regret - due to the use of In Via or the victory from its use suggests sheer folly of its use.

Similar to the moral of the story of King Midas's wish or vain prayer for the 'golden touch'; a wish/prayer that could have led to his starvation as he was left unable to eat with his hands; a wish or prayer that turned that most precious to him, his daughter, into solid gold upon his loving embrace; be careful what you wish/pray for.

NEVER EMPLOY, IN VIA, WITHOUT A TRULY PROLONGED AND THOROUGH DELIBERATION BETWEEN YOU AND THE MOTHER ABOUT ITS USE, AS WELL AS THE REASON FOR ITS USE.

THE REVELATIONS
OF THE TRULY CONNECTED

★ *After you've been awarded victory through your use of, In Via/The Way —*
★ *Following the effectuation of the miracle granted to you through its use —*
★ *Write down what new and different techniques have been revealed to your mind — techniques that would make the use of, In Via/The Way even more effective and efficient.*

That's what this section is about - revelations -
specifically recording yours.

As practitioners of In Via — we are now on the same path, and as you journey onward, you not only progress in the practice itself, you progress wholly.
Some students go on to become even better teachers. They take the techniques they've learned, ones that have worked and served them well, and add to them, or they create new ones that are even more effective. (See: 3rd ★ above)

As a son and pupil, I was taught and encouraged to use, by my father, even before my birth, REVELATION. - Its meaning, its power, and its importance need to be and must be, understood.

*Revelation: **1. Something that is revealed, especially something surprising. 2. An act of revealing.***
That is (according to the American Heritage Dictionary definition) what revelation means. I've also explained earlier that revelation is one way God speaks to you. Thus, it should be evident that revelations' power and importance are paramount!

Furthermore, consider this —

It is my opinion that — all religious concepts, ideas, instructions, rituals, etcetera, given to man so that he fully connects to the source, whether in life or death, were all born initially of divine revelation. *Through deep meditation, dreams within prolonged sleep, or the deepening connection with oneself through total/complete and protracted isolation, some universal truths revealed themselves to the ones seeking them.*

However —

Divine Revelation is not an occurrence or an ability strictly reserved for prophets.

Remember now the connection we share. - As a dedicated practitioner of, In Via — though even without being so — YOU, just as any of human history's mightiest prophets have done, can have all the same wisdom, power, and glory of the universe, shared/revealed entirely and directly to you; instilled forever within you. Ergo, now that you are truly connected and have accepted the truth *and the* reality *of,* The Way *(See: 3rd ★ above)*

— Allow me to share one last essential and just as relevant thought with you.

All that you have read, from the cover to this point and until the end of this manual, has been revealed to me through *my* connection with, The Divine Energy. It is a true *revelation* of divine order. However, although all that I've written, explained, expressed, and impressed upon you, is the *truth* as I know it, *universal truth* as revealed to me, it is still just "one small part"; just another way of tapping into the universal power that connects all living things.

Moreover, In Via, as revealed to me, should be considered my personal and particular *belief. That means, according* to the American Heritage Dictionary definition of "Belief", it is, though 100% honest, simply my **opinion. — this is the Veejay Steele version of In Via**.
> (Belief: 1. Trust or confidence. 2. A conviction or opinion. 3. A tenet or body of tenets.)

I am also aware that some books containing very similar teachings, information, and stories are (by most of the people in the groups that fully subscribe to those texts) considered to be and thought to contain - *total truth and facts ONLY*. Some of these books even suggest that their texts and practices are **the <u>only</u> way** to obtain a meaningful connection; oneness; spiritual enlightenment; with or through, The Almighty; a serious proposition that is both correct and incorrect at the same time. How so? Well, do they contain TRUTH? Yes, we *believe* so. Yet, *all* these practices/religions will set you on a path that leads to the same destination; some, honestly, even without being strictly followed.

Furthermore, and even more importantly, is the fact that anything that is in any way connected to *'belief'* is, by definition, simply an *opinion*. That's all ANY of this, ALL OF IT, is on that account—some persons' opinions. You having faith, your *belief* in their words, in the word, is you sharing that *opinion*.

Even still —
There should be no mistaking that there exists genuine value in ALL of the written works of this type.

As for In Via/The Way —
> I wrote this particular text as if it were an instruction manual — similar to that for a new home theater or audio system.
> - **You open it, and you see the *parts*.**
> - **You must learn the parts to assemble it more easily.**
> - **Afterward, you still need to know how to *operate* it.**
> - **It's new, very high-tech, and difficult to understand how to use it. However, once you've put it together — WOW!!!! It produces/creates such beautiful music! It's so clear! It delivers a sound quality that was unheard of before.**

You already know that there are other books (much older books, books that are part of tested, tried, and true ways of life) that once you've followed the instructions, you will reap the rewards in the end. In other words, they will produce wonderful music for you; this is why it shouldn't matter if your instruction manual is much older and helps put together for you a victrola; or if it's, In Via - a manual for this state-of-the-art, exceedingly powerful, audio or theater system. - In the end, they produce the music you want to hear.

PERSONAL REVELATION
of
Veejay Steele

My use of The Way has culminated in what I can only describe as an ascension into true ONENESS with The Mother. As a result, what I needed to be done, was done; but only because my highest thoughts and desires became The Mother's WILL. - ***HER WILL BE DONE.***
Not even the power of '*choice*' can keep The Mother's WILL from being done.

God's WILL **CANNOT** be defied nor denied.

Again, what I needed to be done was done because it is the will of God; through ascension to true ONENESS, MY *thoughts* became HER *will*.

★ *There is NOTHING more powerful than her will; nothing exists, can, or will ever exist that can prevent or hinder - the will of God.*

Amen.

Thank you for allowing me to share this with you.
Sylvester (Veejay) F. Steele Jr.

Please understand —
I honestly believe that all I've shared with you is FACT; it is REALITY.
However, reality is just the opinion of the person(s) to whom that reality belongs.

A VERY SPECIAL THANKS & PERSONAL NOTE:

Thanks, big bruh (Kal-El Scipio Spencer), for asking me, "Vee, what do you believe?";
and insisting I explain it in as much detail as possible.
Kal, you know that conversation & the ones that followed are why I thought to write it all
down in the first place.

However, it's also true that "In Via" would have NEVER been written if it were not a
proven practice — if the victory I sought wasn't awarded to me. The only way I'd push
this, the only way I'd be willing to share it with anyone, with the world, was if it worked for
me. - I needed proof of my own.

I'm wearing it on my sleeve when I say —

I was going through more pain and suffering than I could have imagined. An emotional
turmoil that left me wanting to/planning to take my own life.
I turned to The Way (In Via). I used it as I knew I should, as I knew I could, and was,
eventually, given the victory I sought. I was granted a miracle that, as I think on it now,
makes NO SENSE WHATSOEVER that it happened! I then committed fully to writing this
manual; to share with you my acceptance of what I've always known to be true. What
was proven to me, without a doubt, to be; THE WAY things are; THE WAY things work;
THE WAY to proceed to ensure total and divine victory; THE WAY to triumph.

GLOSSARY:

(glossary entries are as the words appear in the manual; however, definitions may be that of their root word)

- ❖ **Accentuation** (American Heritage Dictionary): Accentuate [verb:] Accentuated - Accentuating 1. To accent {verb: to stress; emphasize].

- ❖ **Adversarial** (Google Dictionary): [adjective:] 1. Involving or characterized by conflict or opposition.: "Industry and government had an adversarial relationship".

- ❖ **Amidst** (American Heritage Dictionary): Amid or Amidst [preposition:] 1. In the middle of; among.

- ❖ **Assembly** (American Heritage Dictionary): [noun: plural] Assemblies 1. The act of assembling or the state of being assembled. 2. A group of persons gathered together for a common purpose. 3. Assembly. The lower house of legislature. 4a. The putting together of parts to make a completed product. 4b. A set of parts so assembled: the steering assembly of a truck. 5. The signal calling troops to assemble.

- ❖ **Apostle** (American Heritage Dictionary): [noun:] 1. One of the 12 disciples chosen by Christ to preach the gospel. 2. One who leads a cause.
- ❖ **Apostle** (Veejay Steele): High-ranking official of, Triumph The Church And Kingdom of God In Christ.

- ❖ **Ascending** (American Heritage Dictionary): [verb:] 1. To go or move upward; rise. 2. To come to occupy: ascended the throne.

- ❖ **Ascension** (American Heritage Dictionary): [noun:] 1. The act or process of ascending. 2. Ascension. The bodily ascent of Christ into heaven, celebrated on the 40th day after Easter.

- ❖ **Belief** (American Heritage Dictionary): [noun:] 1. Trust or confidence. 2. A conviction or opinion. 3. A tenet or a body of tenets.
- ❖ **Belief** (Veejay Steele): used for and due to its importance as a synonym for; faith, opinion, and sentiment, as stated/written in the American Heritage Dictionary - Roget's II: The New Thesaurus.

- ❖ **Bishop** (American Heritage Dictionary): [noun:] 1. A high-ranking Christian clergyman, usu. In charge of a diocese. 2. A chessman that can move diagonally across any number of unoccupied spaces of the same color.

- ❖ **Catalyst** (American Heritage Dictionary): [noun:] 1. A substance that modifies and especially increases the rate of a chemical reaction without being consumed in the process.
- ❖ **Catalyst** (Veejay Steele): used as another way to say, "to bring about" or "to give rise to" {with *rise* itself meaning: source or origin of.: "It was here that freethinking had its rise".

- ❖ **Cerebral** (American Heritage Dictionary): [adjective:] 1. Of or pertaining to the brain or cerebrum.

- ❖ **Conception** (American Heritage Dictionary): [noun:] 1. The fusing of a sperm and egg to form a zygote capable of developing into a new organism. 2. A beginning; start. 3. The ability to form or understand mental concepts. 4. A concept, plan, design, or thought.

- ❖ **Credence** (American Heritage Dictionary): [noun:] 1. Acceptance as true; belief.
- ❖ **Credence** (Apple Inc. version 2.2.1 Dictionary 2005-2016): [noun:] 1. Belief in or acceptance of something as true: psychoanalysis finds little credence among laymen. • the likelihood of something being true; plausibility: being called upon by the media as an expert lends credence to one's opinions. 2. [usually as modifier] A small side table, shelf, or niche in a church for holding the elements of the Eucharist before they are consecrated: a credence table.

- ❖ **Cynic** (American Heritage Dictionary): [noun:] 1. One who believes all people are motivated by selfishness.

- ❖ **Deliberation** (American Heritage Dictionary): [noun:] 1. Careful consideration. 2. Often deliberations. Careful discussion of an issue.

- ❖ **Derived** (American Heritage Dictionary): [verb:] Derived - Deriving 1. To obtain or issue from a source. 2. To deduce; infer. 3. To trace the origin or development of. 4. To produce or obtain (a compound) from another substance by chemical reaction.

- ❖ **Detrimental** (American Heritage Dictionary): [noun:] 1. Damage, harm, or loss. 2. Something that causes damage, harm, or loss.

- ❖ **Diminish** (American Heritage Dictionary): [verb:] 1. To make or become smaller or less important. 2. To taper.

- ❖ **Diminutive** (American Heritage Dictionary): [adjective:] 1. Of very small size; tiny. 2. Expressing smallness or affection, as the suffix -let in booklet. [noun:] 1. A diminutive suffix, word, or name.

- ❖ **Divine** (American Heritage Dictionary): (1) [adjective:] Diviner - Divinest 1. Being or having the nature of a deity. 2. Of or relating to a deity. 3. Superhuman; godlike. 4. Supremely good; magnificent. [noun:] 1. A clergyman. 2. A theologian. (2) [verb:] Divined - Divining 1. To foretell or prophesy. 2. To guess, infer, or conjecture.

- ❖ **Doctrine** (American Heritage Dictionary): [noun:] 1. Something that is taught. 2. A tenet; dogma.

- ❖ **Dogma** (American Heritage Dictionary): [noun:] 1. A system of doctrines proclaimed by a church. 2. A principle or system of principles.

- ❖ **Earnest** (American Heritage Dictionary): (1) [adjective:] 1. Serious and determined. 2. Showing or expressing deep sincerity or feeling. 3. Of an important nature; grave. [idioms:] In earnest 1. With serious purpose or intent. Earnest (2) [noun:] 1. something, as money paid in advance, given by a purchaser to a seller to bind a contract.

- ❖ **Effectuation** (American Heritage Dictionary): [verb:] Effectuated - Effectuating 1. To bring about; effect.
- ❖ **Effectuation** (Apple Inc. version 2.2.1 Dictionary 2005-2016): [verb:] [with object] formal 1. Put into force or operation: school choice would effectuate a transfer of power from government to individuals. [DERIVATIVES:] effectuation |əˌfek(t)SHəˈwāSH(ə)n| noun

- ❖ **Employ** (American Heritage Dictionary): [verb:] 1. To engage or use the services of. 2. To put to service; use. 3. To devote or apply (one's time or energies) to an activity. [noun:] 1. Employment.

- ❖ **Enacted** (Apple Inc. version 2.2.1 Dictionary 2005-2016): [verb:] [with object] 1. Make (a bill or other proposal) law: legislation was enacted in 1987 to attract international companies. • put into practice (a belief, idea, or suggestion). 2. Act out (a role or play) on stage.

- ❖ **Energy** (Google Dictionary): [noun:] 1. The strength and vitality required for sustained physical or mental activity.: "Changes in the levels of vitamins can affect energy and well-being". 2. Power derived from the utilization of physical or chemical resources, especially to provide light and heat or to work machines. 3. The property of matter and radiation that is manifest as a capacity to perform work (such as causing motion or the interaction of molecules).: "a collision in which no energy is transferred".
- ❖ **Energy** (American Heritage Dictionary): [noun: plural] Energies 1. The work that a physical system is capable of doing in changing from its actual state to a specified reference state. 2. Capacity for action or accomplishment. 3. Strength and vigor; force.
- ❖ **Energy** (Veejay Steele): First, understand that it is my opinion/belief that the essence and energy of God are inseparable; I believe the other should be implied when speaking of either. Thus, I sometimes refer to the power/force emitting from the spirit and our essence when I speak of energy. This energy exists because of our spirit/essence, and our spirit/essence exists because of this energy (know God - know You).
- ❖ **Energy** (Energy: Defining - from Wikipedia): Because energy exists in many interconvertible forms, and yet can't be created or destroyed, its measurement may be equivalently "defined" and quantified via its transfer or conversions into various forms… …

- ❖ **Equivalently** (American Heritage Dictionary): [adverb:] 1. Equal. 2. Almost identical in function or effect.

- ❖ **Ergo** (American Heritage Dictionary): [adverb & conjunction:] 1. Consequently; therefore.

- ❖ **Essence** (American Heritage Dictionary): [noun:] 1. The intrinsic or indispensable properties of a thing. 2. A concentrated extract of a substance that retains its fundamental properties. 3. A perfume.

- ❖ **Faith** (American Heritage Dictionary): [noun:] 1a. Confident belief; trust. 1b. Belief in God; religious conviction. 2. Loyalty; allegiance. 3. A religion.

- ❖ **Flock** (American Heritage Dictionary): [noun:] 1. A group of animals, like birds or sheep, that live, travel or feed together. 2. A group of people under the leadership of one person. 3. A large crowd or number. [verb:] 1. To congregate or travel in a flock or crowd.
- ❖ **Flock** (Veejay Steele): those (people/persons) who are uninterested in standing out, taking the lead, or advancing beyond what has been or is being taught to them.

- ❖ **Forthwith** (American Heritage Dictionary): [adverb:] 1. At once; immediately.

- ❖ **Frequency** (American Heritage Dictionary): [noun: plural] Frequencies 1. The number of occurrences of a specified event within a given interval, as 1a. The number of complete cycles of a wave that occurs within a period of time. 1b. The number of complete oscillations or vibrations that a body undergoes in a given period of time. 2. The condition of occurring repeatedly at short intervals.
- ❖ **Frequency** (Google Dictionary): [noun:] 1. The rate at which something occurs or is repeated over a particular period of time or in a given sample.: "shops have closed with increasing frequency during the period". 2. The rate at which a vibration occurs that constitutes a wave, either in a material (as in sound waves), or in an electromagnetic field (as in radio waves and light), usually measured per second.

❖ **Gestation** (American Heritage Dictionary): [noun:] 1. The period of carrying developing offspring in the uterus after conception; pregnancy.

❖ **Habituation** (Google Dictionary): [noun:] 1. The action of habituating or the condition of being habituated.

❖ **Habituation** (Apple Inc. version 2.2.1 Dictionary 2005-2016): [noun:] 1. The action of habituating or the condition of being habituated. • Psychology: the diminishing of a physiological or emotional response to a frequently repeated stimulus.

❖ **Harnessing** (American Heritage Dictionary): [noun:] 1. Gear by which a draft animal pulls a vehicle or implement. [verb:] 1. To put a harness on. 2. To control and direct the force of. [idioms:] in harness 1. Engaged in one's usual work.

❖ **Hither** (American Heritage Dictionary): [adverb:] 1. To or toward this place: come hither. [adjective:] 1. Located on the near side.

❖ **Immeasurable** (American Heritage Dictionary): [adjective:] 1. Incapable of being measured. 2. Vast; limitless.

❖ **Implied** (American Heritage Dictionary): [verb:] 1. To involve or suggest by logical necessity; entail. 2. To express indirectly; suggest without stating.

❖ **Inauspicious** (American Heritage Dictionary): [adjective:] 1. Not auspicious; unfavorable.

❖ **Indivisible** (American Heritage Dictionary): [adjective:] 1. Incapable of being divided.

❖ **Induce** (American Heritage Dictionary): [verb:] Induced - Inducing 1. To prevail upon; persuade or influence. 2. To stimulate the occurrence of; cause: induce childbirth. 3. To infer by inductive reasoning.

❖ **Infinite** (American Heritage Dictionary): [adjective:] 1. Having no bounds or limits; endless. 2. Immeasurably great or large; immense. 3. Mathematics. 3a. Existing beyond or being greater than any arbitrarily large value. 3b. Unlimited in spatial extent.

❖ **Innate** (American Heritage Dictionary): [adjective:] 1. Possessed at birth; inborn. 2. Possessed as an essential characteristic; inherent.

❖ **Inseparable** (American Heritage Dictionary): [adjective:] 1. Incapable of being separated.

❖ **Intelligence** (American Heritage Dictionary): [noun:] 1a. The capacity to acquire and apply knowledge. 1b. The faculty of thought and reason. 1c. Superior powers of mind. 2. Received information; news. 3a. Secret information, especially about an enemy. 3b. The work of gathering such information.

❖ **Interconvertible** (English Oxford Dictionary): [adjective:] see interconvert: **Interconvert** [verb] (with object) 1. Cause two things to be converted into each other.

❖ **Interference** (American Heritage Dictionary): [verb:] Interfered - Interfering 1. To hinder; impede. 2. Sports: to impede illegally the catching of a pass or the playing of a ball or puck. 3. To intervene or intrude in the affairs of others; meddle. 4. To inhibit or prevent clear reception of broadcast signals.

- ❖ **Manual** (American Heritage Dictionary): [adjective:] 1. Of, pertaining to, or operated by the hands. 2. Requiring physical rather than mental effort. [noun:] 1. A small book of instructions. 2. Military: prescribed movements in the handling of a weapon.

- ❖ **Meticulous** (American Heritage Dictionary): [adjective:] 1. Extremely or excessively careful and precise: a meticulous worker.

- ❖ **Morality** (American Heritage Dictionary): [noun: plural] Moralities 1. The quality of being moral. 2. A system of conduct based on principles of right and wrong. 3. Virtuous conduct.

- ❖ **Negative** (American Heritage Dictionary): [adjective:] 1. Expressing negation, refusal, or denial. 2. Not positive or constructive: negative criticism. 3. Pertaining to or denoting a quantity less than zero or a quantity, number, angle, velocity, or direction in a sense opposite to another indicated or understood to be positive. 4. Pertaining to or denoting electric charge of the same sign as that of an electron, designated by the symbol (-). [noun:] 1. A negative word, statement, or concept. 2. The side opposing the opinion upheld by the affirmative side in a debate. 3a. An image in which the light areas of the object rendered appear dark and the dark areas appear light. 3b. A film, plate, or other photographic material containing such an image. [verb:] negatived - negativing 1. To refuse to approve; veto. 2. To deny; contradict.

- ❖ **Ominous** (American Heritage Dictionary): [adjective:] 1. Being or pertaining to an evil omen; foreboding; portentous. 2. Menacing; threatening.

- ❖ **Opinion** (American Heritage Dictionary): [noun:] 1. A belief held often without positive knowledge or proof. 2. An evaluation based on special knowledge. 3. A judgment or estimation.

- ❖ **Positive** (American Heritage Dictionary): [adjective:] 1. Characterized by or displaying affirmation: a positive answer. 2. Explicitly expressed: a positive demand. 3. Admitting of no doubt; irrefutable. 4. Certain; confident. 5. Real and not fictitious. 6. Pertaining to or designating: 6a a quantity greater than zero. 6b a quantity, number, angle, or direction opposite to another designated as negative. [noun:] 1. A photographic image in which the lights and darks appear as they do in nature. 2. Grammar: the positive degree of an adjective or adverb.

- ❖ **Practitioner** (American Heritage Dictionary): [noun:] 1. One who practices an occupation, profession, or technique.

- ❖ **Praxis** (Google Dictionary): [noun:] 1. Practice, as distinguished from theory.: "the gap between theory and praxis, text and world".

- ❖ **Presentiment** (American Heritage Dictionary): [noun:] 1. A sense of something about to occur; premonition.

- ❖ **Propagating** (American Heritage Dictionary): [verb:] Propagated - Propagating 1. To reproduce or cause to reproduce; breed. 2. To make known; publicize. 3. Physics: to move or cause to move through a medium.

- ❖ **Protracted** (American Heritage Dictionary): [verb:] 1. To draw out; prolong.

- ❖ **Proverbial** (American Heritage Dictionary): [noun:] 1. A short, popular saying expressing a well-known truth or fact. 2. Proverbs. (used with a singular verb) a book of the bible.

❖ **Proverbial** (Google Dictionary): [adjective:] 1. (of a word or phrase) referred to in a proverb or idiom.: "I'm going to stick out like the proverbial sore thumb".

❖ **Reality** (American Heritage Dictionary): [noun: plural] Realities 1. The condition or quality of being real or true. 2. Something that is real.

❖ **Rigmarole** (Google Dictionary): [noun:] 1. A lengthy and complicated procedure.: "he went through the rigmarole of securing the front door".
❖ **Rigmarole** (American Heritage Dictionary - Roget's II: The New Thesaurus): stuff - nonsense - bilge - trash - idiocy - balderdash - blather - bunkum - claptrap - drivel - eyewash - piffle - poppycock - tomfoolery - twaddle.

❖ **Sanctity** (American Heritage Dictionary): [noun: plural] Sanctities 1. Holiness of life; saintliness. 2. Sacredness or inviolability: the sanctity of the family.

❖ **Sheep** (American Heritage Dictionary): [noun: plural] 1. A hoofed, thick-fleeced mammal widely domesticated for wool and meat. 2. One who is meek and submissive.

❖ **Signature** (American Heritage Dictionary): [noun:] 1. The name of a person as written by that person. 2. A distinctive mark, characteristic, or sound effect. 3. A symbol on a musical staff used to indicate tempo.

❖ **Sinister** (American Heritage Dictionary): [adjective:] 1. Suggesting an evil force or motive. 2. Promising trouble; ominous.

❖ **Stifle** (American Heritage Dictionary): [verb:] Stifled - Stifling 1. To kill by preventing respiration; smother. 2. To keep or hold back; suppress. 3. To die of suffocation.

❖ **Subservient** (American Heritage Dictionary): [adjective:] 1. Subordinate. 2. Obsequious; servile.

❖ **Symbiosis** (American Heritage Dictionary): [noun:] 1. Biology: the relationship or living together of two or more different organisms in a close association, especially when mutually beneficial.

❖ **Tenet** (American Heritage Dictionary): [noun:] 1. A fundamental principle or dogma.

❖ **Theological** (American Heritage Dictionary): [noun:] 1. The study of the nature of God and religious truth. 2. An organized body of opinions concerning God and man's relationship to God.

❖ **Theoretically** (American Heritage Dictionary): Theory [noun: plural] Theories 1. A statement or set of statements designed to explain a phenomenon or class of phenomena. 2. A set of rules or principles designed for the study or practice of an art or discipline. 3. Abstract thought untested in practice. 4. An assumption or guess.

❖ **Thereon** (American Heritage Dictionary): [adverb:] 1. On or upon that or it. 2. Following that immediately.

❖ **Tribulations** (American Heritage Dictionary): [noun:] 1. Great affliction or distress. 2. Something that causes such distress.

❖ **Unequivocal** (American Heritage Dictionary): [adjective:] 1. Not open to doubt or misunderstanding; clear.

- ❖ **Yin-Yang** (Yin and Yang, From Wikipedia, the free encyclopedia): Literal meaning: dark – bright. In Chinese philosophy, yin and yang (also *yin–yang* or *yin yang*, 陰陽 *yīnyáng* "dark–bright") describe how seemingly opposite or contrary forces may actually be complementary, interconnected, and interdependent in the natural world, and how they may give rise to each other as they interrelate to one another.

- ❖ **Zeal** (American Heritage Dictionary): [noun:] 1. Enthusiastic and diligent devotion, as to a cause, ideal, or goal; ardor.

ILLUSTRATION INDEX:

(the photocopies of the images {artwork & photos used or created for this manual] in order of their appearance)

(FRONT COVER)

"FRONT COVER" is the hand-painted interpretation of "*The Way*", designed & created by, Akiya L. Anderson-Steele, A.K.A. Akiya Steele. *It was created to be the front cover of, In Via/The Way.

[PROGRAMS/SOFTWARE: Preview.app, GIMP, & Fotor Photo Editor, and the online program/app Google Slides were used by Veejay Steele to modify/alter photos to create the final front & back cover.]

(THE MOTHER)

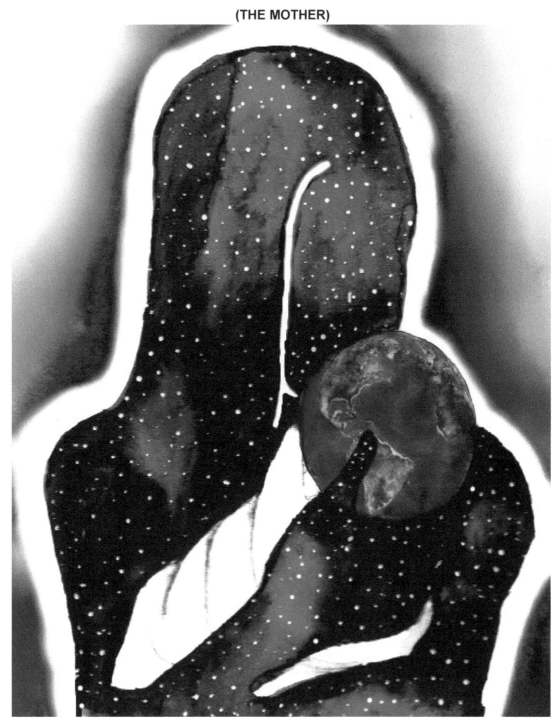

Found in ~ <u>Section I: PARTS, (A) - God:</u> ~ "THE MOTHER", is the watercolor hand painting of
'God/The Source/The divine Energy, as the nurturer of a baby planet Earth',
by Akiya L. Anderson-Steele

★ ABOUT THE CREATIVE CONTROL GIVEN TO THE ARTIST:

After reading "In Via", Akiya, decided where - any & all - illustrations were needed. As well as what they should look like or depict. It was left entirely up to her: when, where, and if any illustration were to be used throughout this book. Thus, FRONT COVER, like every other illustration within the book, is the artist's interpretation of the subject and what she feels the message in the portion of the text that she has decided to illustrate is trying to convey.

(YOU ARE GOD)

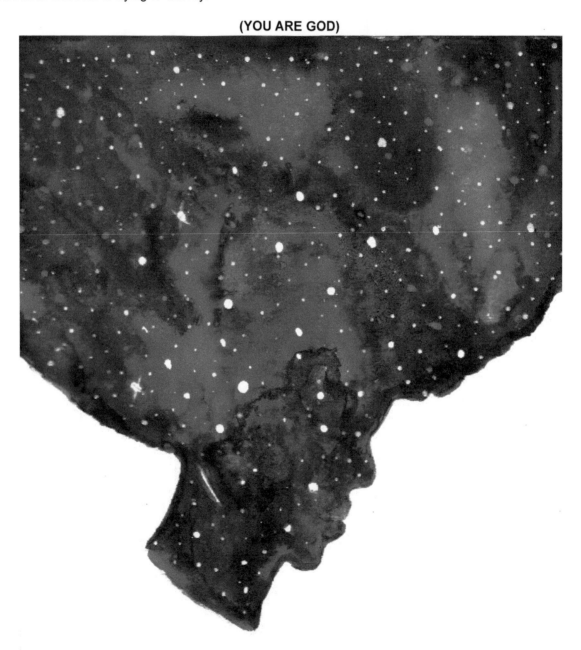

Found in ~ <u>Section I: PARTS, (B) - You:</u> ~ "YOU ARE GOD", is the watercolor hand painting of '*Man as God & God as a man*', by Akiya L. Anderson-Steele

(THE SIGNAL)

Found in ~ <u>Section I: PARTS, (C) - Connection:</u> ~ "THE SIGNAL", is the watercolor hand painting of '*an individual radio tower emitting its particular signal*', by Akiya Steele.

(STEP 1)

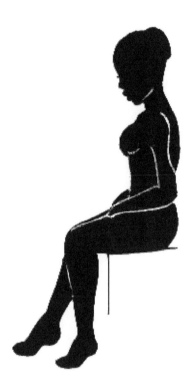

Found in ~ <u>Section II: ASSEMBLY,</u> <u>Step 1</u> - ~ "STEP 1", is the hand-drawn illustration of '*sitting and preparing to establish a connection to The Divine Energy; to The Universe; to The Source; to The Creator; to God; to Her*', by Akiya L. Anderson-Steele.

(STEP 2)

Found in ~ <u>Section II: ASSEMBLY, Step 2 -</u> ~ "STEP 2", is the hand-drawn illustration of '*one particular form of communing (in progress) with The Universe, The Divine Energy, The Force, God*', by Akiya L. Anderson-Steele.

(HARNESS)

Found in ~ <u>Section III: OPERATION</u> ~ "HARNESS", is the hand-drawn illustration of '*harnessing your thoughts*', by Akiya L. Anderson-Steele.

(CEREBRAL LOBES)

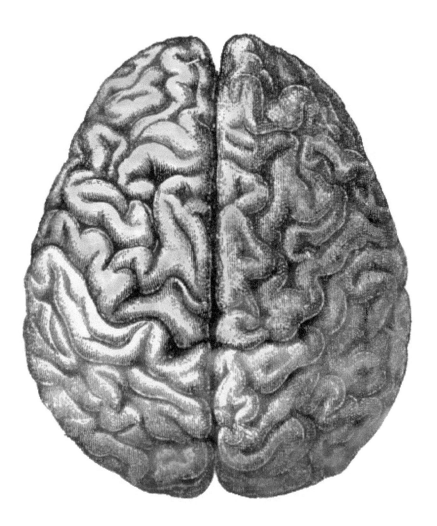

"Human Brain." *Wikipedia*, Wikimedia Foundation, 12 July 2018,
en.wikipedia.org/wiki/Human_brain.

"CEREBRAL LOBES", was used to create the back cover image. The final image,
"Mind Birthing New Stars," was created by, Veejay Steele.

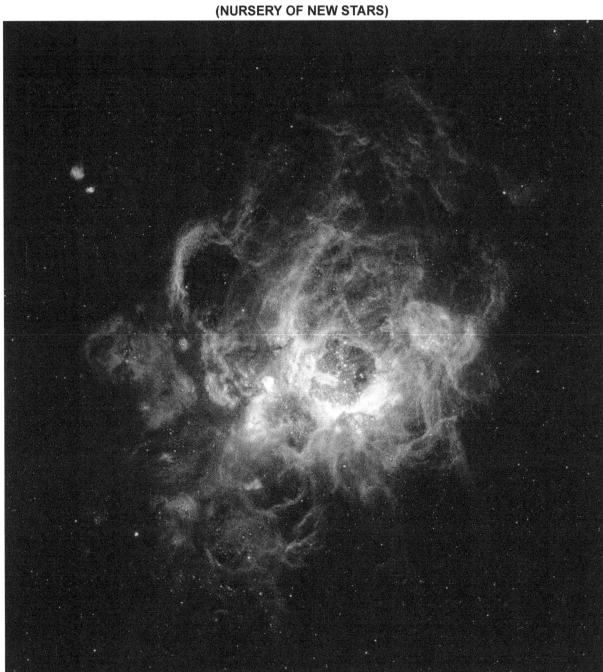

(NURSERY OF NEW STARS)

Wikipedia,
en.wikipedia.org/wiki/File:Nursery_of_New_Stars_-_GPN-2000-000972.jpg#/media/File:Nursery_of_
New_Stars_-_GPN-2000-000972.jpg.
[PUBLIC DOMAIN]

"Nursery of New Stars", was used to create the back cover image. The final image,
"Mind Birthing New Stars," was created by, Veejay Steele.

(SYLVESTER F. "VEEJAY" STEELE, JR.)

Veejay - is the entertainer/performer (RAP artist, singer, songwriter, voice actor, author, actor) known as, DecaGon, also known as, -Gon, or, Deca-Gon

(DECAGON AKA -GON, OR, DECA-GON)

NOTES:

Printed in the USA
CPSIA information can be obtained
at www.ICGtesting.com
LVHW071730300824
789716LV00014B/64